LIVES
AND
TIMES

Harriet Tubman

John Rowley

Heinemann
LIBRARY

First published in Great Britain by Heinemann Library
Halley Court, Jordan Hill, Oxford OX2 8EJ,
a division of Reed Educational and Professional Publishing Ltd.

OXFORD FLORENCE PRAGUE MADRID ATHENS
MELBOURNE AUCKLAND KUALA LUMPUR SINGAPORE TOKYO
IBADAN NAIROBI KAMPALA JOHANNESBURG GABORONE
PORTSMOUTH NH (USA) CHICAGO MEXICO CITY SAO PAULO

Designed by Ken Vail Graphic Design, Cambridge
Illustrations by Sean Victory
Printed and bound in Malaysia by Times Offset (M) Sdn. Bhd.

01 00 99 98 97
10 9 8 7 6 5 4 3 2 1

ISBN 0 431 02470 7

Some words are shown in bold, **like this**.
You can find out what they mean by looking
in the glossary. The glossary also helps you
say difficult words.

British Library Cataloguing in Publication Data

Rowley, John
Harriet Tubman. – (Lives & times)
1. Tubman, Harriet, 1821-1913 - Juvenile literature
2. Afro-American women civil rights workers - Biography - Juvenile literature
3. Afro-American civil rights workers - Biography - Juvenile literature
4. Slaves - United States - Biography - Juvenile literature
I. Title
306.3'62'092

Acknowledgements
The Publishers would like to thank the following for permission to reproduce photographs:
Honeywell, Chris, p.21; Hulton Deutsch, pp.18–19;
Schlesinger Library, Radcliffe College, p.22; Sophia Smith Collection, pp.16–17.

Cover photograph: Sophia Smith Collection

Our thanks to Betty Root for her comments in the preparation of this book.

Every effort has been made to contact copyright holders of any material reproduced in this book.
Any omissions will be rectified in subsequent printings if notice is given to the Publisher.

Contents

The first part of this book tells you the story of
Harriet Tubman.
The second part tells you how we can find out
about her life.

Harriet Tubman

This is the story of a very special person called Harriet Tubman. Harriet was a real woman. This is a true story.

Harriet was born in Maryland, America in 1821, about 180 years ago. Harriet's grandparents were born in Africa.

Family

Harriet's family lived on a **plantation**. She had ten brothers and sisters. They all had to work for the man who owned the plantation.

Harriet's family were not allowed to leave the plantation. They had to do what they were told. They were all **slaves**.

Work

When Harriet was six, she had to start work. She never went to school. She worked all day in the fields. She was always very tired.

The **plantation** owner was very bad. He
hit people to make them work harder.
Once, Harriet tried to stop him hitting
someone. He broke her **skull**.

Escape

When Harriet was 28, she ran away. She went to another part of America where people did not have **slaves**.

She found a job in a hotel, but was not
happy. She kept thinking about her family.
She decided to go back to rescue them.

Rescue

It was very dangerous for Harriet to go back to the **plantation**. She had to **disguise** herself so no-one would know who she was. She was very brave.

Harriet made 19 journeys. She **smuggled** out 300 people who had been **slaves**. She moved them through a secret network of safe hiding places. This was known as the **Underground Railroad**.

Freedom

From 1861 to 1865, when Harriet was quite old, there was a war to free all the **slaves**. Harriet helped. First of all, she became a **spy**. Then she became a nurse.

When Harriet was an old woman, she
helped look after the people she rescued.
She bought a big house for them to live in.

Photographs

We know that Harriet was a real person. This is a photograph of her with some of the people she helped. She is the woman on the left of the photograph.

There are no photographs of Harriet as a young girl. We have to guess what she looked like.

This is a photograph of a **plantation**. It was like the plantation that Harriet lived on when she was young. It helps us learn what her life was like.

You can see the **slaves** working in the field and the plantation owner watching over them. This picture shows us how hard the work was.

Books

Harriet could not read or write. Remember, she never went to school. When Harriet was an old lady, she told her story to a friend called Sarah.

Sarah wrote down what Harriet told her. This page is from Sarah's book. The book tells us about Harriet's life.

HARRIET TUBMAN.

Harriet Tubman
THE MOSES OF HER PEOPLE

by Sarah Bradford

Introduction by Butler A. Jones

THE CITADEL PRESS
Secaucus, New Jersey

Pictures and memorials

Harriet was 93 when she died. She was a very important person. People wanted to remember her.

"In memory of Harriet Tubman, called the Moses of her people. With rare courage she led over 500 black people up from slavery to freedom and rendered invaluable service as nurse and spy in the war. She braved every danger and overcame every obstacle. Withal she possessed extraordinary foresight and judgement so that she truthfully said – 'On my Underground Railroad I never ran my train off the track and I never lost a passenger".

The people she had helped decided to make a special sign. They put it on her house. They did not want anyone to forget Harriet Tubman. Can you see her name?

Glossary

This glossary explains difficult words, and helps you to say words which may be hard to say.

disguise dressing up so people do not know who you are. You say *dis-gize*

memorial something which makes you remember a special person – for example, it might be a carved stone, a bench with something written on it or a building. You say *meMORial*

plantation big farm. You say *plan-tay-shun*

skull the bones in your head

slave a person who is forced to work for another person and is never free

smuggling hiding something to get it past a person without them seeing it

spy a person who finds out secrets

Underground Railroad the network of secret places where escaping slaves hid. It was not a real railroad, but the hiding places were called stations and the routes between them lines

Index